An Angel of the First Degree

An Angel of the First Degree

Fifty Years of Love Poems 1970–2020

JAMES A. ZOLLER

RESOURCE *Publications* · Eugene, Oregon

AN ANGEL OF THE FIRST DEGREE
Fifty Years of Love Poems 1970–2020

Resource Publications
An Imprint of Wipf and Stock Publishers
199 W. 8th Ave., Suite 3
Eugene, OR 97401

www.wipfandstock.com

PAPERBACK ISBN: 978-1-7252-8061-8
HARDCOVER ISBN: 978-1-7252-8062-5
EBOOK ISBN: 978-1-7252-8063-2

Manufactured in the U.S.A.   07/20/20

Dedication

For You

This is my heart.
Words will not express it.

These are my hands.
They are not talented hands
but they tell tales.
Restless pigeons, they fly,
coming and going in great flapping.

They approach you now.
They descend, they sing where
words fail.

This is my head. Solemn beast, great lion
that I imagine myself to be,
king of something.

When words fail
I raise my great head.
The pigeons hop and flutter.
I fill my lungs
With the great resounding wind . . .

From Twenty-Five

She's as sweet as Tupelo Honey
She's an angel of the first degree
She's as sweet as Tupelo Honey
Just like honey, baby, from the bee

—Van Morrison, "Tupelo Honey"

...free to wander wherever they choose
[They] Are traveling together...
On the last leg of a journey they started a long time ago
The arc of a love affair,
Rainbows in the high desert air...

—Paul Simon, "Hearts and Bones"

Contents

Use Me

I have many spools
and I am silk thread
use me, my love
as you need me

From Twenty-five

Taking Root

she has the garden of spring
where everything is related

: the carton of milk
half emptied and left to stink
the cow who follows her
through the woods
with flies in its wet nose and eyes

she is raising stone and brambles
little green arrows in the black mud

on the weathered barn wall
she hangs her three pronged rake
her empty watering can

she lets the screen bang behind her
and the sun sinks
earth crawls beneath its dark blanket

all is quiet
except the stars in their snowy caps

out in the garden
where the ground is still warm
I am taking root among her flowers

from Twenty-five

a love poem

For seven days my lady & I
hobbled on the cobblestones brought from Gloucester
& built a past of damp air
 while the piers stood solid & trim
 beside the empty yachts & quiet
 green water stained with oil, blue circular rainbows.
The stillness we sensed was on the beach
where the new was as old as the baked sand
& numbing white waves. Time
 was on the move in Nantucket;
 the old stores & buildings were
 scraped & sanded & shored up
until they looked newer than the new
houses in their storm-grey shingles &
climbing roses. We touched the ancient
 life in the houses for hire with no locks
 with the gaping screens with the tap
 that belched & hissed, rumbling
 & clanking deep down in the guts of the house,
 before trickling its rust colored blood, like a stain, into the bowl.

I touched her in those days, reached for her
 to set the hands of Time itself
 so her hours matched mine, so the dream
 she had shook me in my sleep
& I woke to find her crying of happiness,
our faces held together in sleep long after the tears
dried & left a damp trail on the pillow.

(June 1970)

4

Aging

take the earthen bowl from the shelf
set it on the brown table

let us hide a morsel in it
to discover at another time

when the future
demands its last meal

from Twenty-Five

Seamless Love

It is the genius of every young man
to feel in and of his young woman
that here he has found something
never before seen, heard, thought, felt,

that this gift which is this young woman
is more precious by far than any gift
ever given in mankind's wonderful
sad history, beyond even the dark

wonders of self awareness. And it
is the gift of every young woman
to feel in and of her young man
that her genius lies in giving her self

to this one who is new and strong
and faithful and her exact other.

From Ash & Embers

Marriage: Prelude, Mystery, & Riddles

1.
stars dim
hearts waken.
toward morning
fog settles over Busan.
beneath a sliver of moon
a rose corona lies upon the hills.

2.
as from three
one
so from two
one
such divine math
the mystery of marriage
embodied
our most obvious
oneness

3.
so—what is
male and female
divine and human
trinity and duet and singularity?

why must
harmony
demand all
mind heart body spirit
earth and eternity?

who would find
whole-ness
in the other,
as one,
finds
completion
in God.

From Ash & Embers

The Evil Rose

> You find yourself . . . with a toy harpoon
> lurching fearfully at the evil rose of poverty.
>
> —JAMES TATE

at the sink, hands in warm water,
you talk of your day:
it has been like this since morning,
the sun now well behind the trees.

you take a pan, dirty from boiled noodles;
a priestess, you immerse and cleanse.

having served its purpose, the pan is laid on the shelf,
blessed and forgotten until it's needed again.

you talk, now, of jobs;
not careers but something to put meat
with the noodles,
dollars to buy blankets for the children's beds.

as you talk, I submerge like a yogi into his trance
into my day, which already had been laid aside:
    to the boxes of shoes in tall rows
        that I lift twelve at a time
        high overhead into tight spaces,
    to the women who leave husbands,
        infants, schools, sinks of warm water
        for the haven of the mill

who grow old sewing cowhide
gluing, snipping, stuffing boxes,
to the grandmothers sitting on little stools
folding little cardboard boxes . . .

so I drift, a lazy bubble,
surfacing at the other side of your conversation,
weary from the day, weary twice from the memory of it,
burdened now with these ambitions.

you pause for response
but all I can muster is a neutral grunt
        the tongue is a dull instrument
        and I fear the poor incision
        of my truer thoughts.

from Twenty-five

Untitled Domestic Poem

in the kitchen
with the drafty floor
the temperature dipped
and I turned on the heat
for the first time since early May

the radiators bang
an old tune I'd forgotten

we fought it
vowed to live in sweaters
long wool underwear

and how we fought it
but this morning
answering the clock in the cold
in the black silk of October
I gave in

moved by the blue of your hands
in the dim light

from Twenty-five

Missing You in Toledo

Outside Toledo where the train has stopped
    to wait for tracks ahead to clear
I record simple observations:
    a red-yellow-green totem
(Bear, eagle, snake)
    faces the tracks,
A refugee in some back yard,
    scanning travelers, anonymous, lost.

From daybreak I note the earth has flattened:
    broad farmland, featureless,
So incredibly black. Between field and tracks
    through a gully, telephone poles,
Globe-wrapping miles of wire
    and voices voices voices
But not yours, not mine.

In back lots abutting the tracks junked stoves,
    refrigerators without doors,
Washing machines orange with rust,
    miles of these stark objects—
The guts of kitchens sluiced into ditches, discarded.

Now the train begins to move,
    the bright puzzling totem slips past.
It is, I know suddenly, an icon,
    fiercely shaped to keep hope alive.

But what, as it reappears on this page, can I tell you
       that might reduce the miles,
The growing gap between us?

I have missed you in Toledo.

from Twenty-five

This is How It Will Be When We Die
Whether You Die First, Or I
(I in San Francisco, You in New York)

I am here, half of me
    working by nerves mostly,
    energy that never fails but

fails to comfort,
    keeps me up late,
    gets you up early,

destroys our natural rhythm—
    the rhythm of voice, of body,
    of response, of time or innerworldly rhyme.

I travel badly when I travel alone.

From Twenty-five

For Valentine's Day (Reason Enough)

It has been a long winter
with more snow and cold
than we have grown used to.

The house grows smaller:
the town shrinks.

News from the outside
    is uniformly disheartening.

But at night we still
climb into the same bed
where all we hold dear we hold in common,
where daily we enact our commitment.

That, finally, is reason enough
to continue.

From Twenty-five

Romance of Air and Bones

Along the dead-end street
you and I walk hand in hand,

listening to the soft snow
drifting through this gray afternoon,

watching flakes light upon
our dark winter clothes.

When you speak,
dark-limbed trees lean in,

the sky brightens.
When you speak, your words

appear in the cold air,
land upon my ears and lashes,

white grows transparent
—your day my day float,

dance in air weightless as snow,
lightened by love and talk

—those ephemeral white crystals,
commonplace of true companions.

From Living on the Flood Plain

18

Let The Earth Be Silent No More

God in His Sanctuary
  surveys all He has brought to pass
Let the earth be silent

Out of darkness
  He brings love

Everything in its time   Dawn,
  The beginning of life, then dusk

Out of chaos
  His hands imagine
  He spins the globe upon His palm
  He orders spring to follow winter
  He taps out rhythm for each beating heart

The hour glass of eternity in every breath

He spills the galaxies
  Into the black void of space
    A trail of sparks

Out of cold
  He raises the sun

Out of silence
  He calls birds to sing
  He gives voice to water
  to the wings of bees
  He tunes the wind in leaves

Out of emptiness
　　He brings abundance
　　He burdens our hands with goodness

Out of woman
　　He brings man

Out of man
　　He brings generations

In the morning
　　We are filled with hope
　　with ambition with energy
On this morning
　　Our hopes are at once realized
　　and renewed

To everything
　　There is a season
　　A time for passion and
　　　A life for *com*passion

The hour glass of eternity in the eyes of the beloved

We know and will know God's goodness

In His time
　　He sends rain to desert places
　　hard ground erupts with blossoms

Let the earth that was silent
　　be silent no more

Let those who have eyes be filled with seeing
Let those with ears attend to hearing

Let those with voices cry Amen
Let those with hands
    embrace this moment

Let the earth sing to its Creator
    to God in His Sanctuary

At the shore the tide begins turning
In the valley, fog lifts
Along the horizon dawn breaks

The season of waiting has ended
The days of preparation are finished
The hour of celebration has arrived

To everything there is a season
For us, your children
This *is* the season for joy and hope
    the beginning of life

This *is* the day the Lord has made
Let all God's people call it *Blessed*

from The Wedding Poems

The Classroom

You will remember this: silence descending with dusk,
    your room ticking like a hot engine.
Faces that enlivened your youth, your morning,
    have worn you out, have gone.

You will remember this: once live-bodies are gone
    heat lingers, heavy with sweat, burdened
        with musk. The air vibrates—chalk-
        board grey from erasures—
the ghost of SAVE THIS still legible
    in the top left corner.

You hear, somewhere down the hall,
    the distant wail of a vacuum.
You hear it rolling up and back, up and back,
    as the overhead lights, mirrored now
        in the wall of windows,
eclipse the last, lingering streaks of dusk—
    day plunged too soon into darkness.

In October, though daylight is reassigned
    to brighten your morning trek,
you arrive too early for sunrise and depart
    long past sunset. You cannot command daylight
        with a prod, a tap on the shoulder,
            its drooping eyes beyond your steely glare.

You must face this just as
you must face the walk to your car,
    kicking through leaves that may have dazzled you

at mid-day, a week ago, or two
that—fallen—blend
into one shuffling slippered sibilant
just as, shhhhhhhh,
you must face, later, the late labors, the reading,
hoping for a tremor beneath boredom,
a hand reaching through the clutter
toward yours.

From Living on the Flood Plain

On the Occasion of Marriage ~ A Triptych

Cairns[1]

Consider the hour when fog lies below first sun.
We find ourselves upon a path, familiar
yet new as morning is new. Patterned
on Creation itself, each morning a new promise,

each calls us to look, to listen. To treasure it.

Fog lingers. Light opens a way. We step forward
trusting light, the path, the living of each step—
our journeys directed by the silent witness of stones.
Stones of our generations. Stones of struggle, of life.

Stone of fences, walls, roadways, of foundations and altars.

Gathered stone. Discarded and scattered, rubble of ice age
picked cleared hauled chosen, one stone worked upon another
boundary stones, memory stones, stonework beside cleared fields.
This stone, faithfulness. That one, endurance. Support. Love.

Paving stones, companion stones, milestones. Cairns.

Quarried stone. Granite, marble. Pillar. Foundation stones
laid and fitted. Cornerstone, stone of reference and alignment.
Witness of design. Direction. Witness of upheaval and weather.
Whetstone, each in turn, for honing tools, talents, character.

---

1. Rough stones piled as memorials or landmarks

Keystone. Conjoining love and faith, the arch of marriage.

Precious stones, gold silver emerald. A woman chosen.
A man refined. A marriage of partners, of character hewn by God.
Adorn your neck with love. Bind it to your wrist, your waist.
Etch faithfulness on the tablet of your hearts.

Trust. Wisdom. Ledge and bedrock. Lodestone. Living stones.

Corona[2]

At the moment sunlight breaks
    along the horizon, fog contracts.
What path you choose to travel
    lies before you, worn and unknown.
What foundations you build on
    have already been laid.

For this hour the whole earth
    lies quietly at your feet.
Its bounty is the bounty
    of love and faithfulness.
Its enduring goodness spills
    as water from God's hands.

The resting stones of the first cairns
    peak through the valley cloud.
The path toward those markers
    dissolves into mist beneath bright skies.
This is the nature of faith's fullness:
    under heaven, one clear step.

In this new air, first light
    glories upon your faces.
It is a nimbus, a bright mantle
    about your shoulders,
A corona of favor and blessing
    as you stand together.

2. The luminous ring around a celestial body visible in haze or thin cloud
    Also, a crown

Commission

God in His great Goodness
fills the earth with wonder

stone for building
wildness for awe
grain and fruit for sustenance
laughter for your hearts' increase

struggle for harnessing strength
children for joy beyond words, for pressing on
children for teaching you of God's nature
for grounding you in your own humanity

talents for nurturing your souls
sorrows that you might treasure each other
virtue that you might know goodness

God in His great Love
fills the earth with mystery

Let love adorn your lives
Let wisdom establish your home
Let faithfulness shine from your skin
a birthmark to be esteemed

Let these three form a trinity of hope

Hold your other's hand in this journey
so that wavering might be steadied

that stumbling might be restored
so that one might lend strength to both
should feet grow dull

so that in the feebleness of age, unimaginable,
that burdens us all at day's end,
fear might be dispelled

For this you have been made and nurtured
For this we have gathered in witness
Walk among us as One
a *new* creation

from The Wedding Poems

This Most Obvious of Things

I am looking, as I leave, for a way
to say I love you, this most obvious of things.

It is mid-October, and I drive through valleys
alone, beneath blue sky both bright and unbroken

driving distractedly, despite my intentions,
slowed every mile by hillside after hillside

of brilliant red leaves, of vivid orange
leaves of shimmering gold against evergreen

as if the unplanned patterns lay like sky
unbroken, the impression of seamless difference

tugging the eyes like water eddying over stones
tugs the ear, thrilling the heart

until breathing is labored and hours
have passed without notice, slipping, gone.

Soon it will be dusk, then dark,
the texture of hillsides gone in darkness

the fabric, the folds of color gone black
as my destination draws nearer.

For a moment the straight western sun, burning
in the treetops, strikes west-facing slopes opposite

setting reds aflame, burnishing gold
until it nearly blinds, warming orange and brown

this whole world filled, unspeakably, with fire.
And I, unsentimental man that I am,

I, who have been looking for a way
who have wanted words for love, for you

who have felt now, my heart opened
and opening, who would bring you here with me

I, who would say *this is what love
must mean*, who would say foolish things

find myself doubly at a loss,
having seen heaven, alone.

From Living on the Flood Plain

Nocturn
(as Frost said)

We have nested among rustlings
as mice nest among leaves.

We become like them, making night noises:
Sonorous respiration, responsive shifting

(choreographed to back-
drop of odd random street rumblings,

hum of freezer, unheard voices
in wires along the streets).

Then we crawl inside sleep among these leafy
sounds. Like the voices in wires

we travel together
as we travel alone.

From Twenty-Five

Getting It Right

In the old farmhouse we have inherited
all the floors need topographical maps.

The bookcases I have made with rigorous angles
lean to the corners like inebriates.

The refrigerator and stove
travel downhill.

What can we learn from all this?
Ignoring our dreams and plans,

love opens many little doors
that we race through imprudently.

From Twenty-Five

On Your Marriage

Like a new day
    is the marriage
of a man and a woman;
    we rise up with joy and greet them.

Like a bright sun
    is marriage before God;
its light calls forth good things
    and makes safe life's paths.

Blessed are they
    who come together in Christ:
wisely have they established their future

    Happy are you
who commit yourselves in love
    to one another.

For this life
    have we raised you;
for this calling
    have we trained you up

Happy are we
    who witness your vows.

From The Wedding Poems

In Praise of Fire

Even in darkness
we find words,

we who know each other,
fellow travelers. Survivors.

My spine carries
the weight of stars;

the skin of my hands
carries icons,

small white scars
without number,

each a miracle of healing
to fill me with praise.

Even in darkness
we know each other,

know the nature
of common blessing;

our sons, grown tall
to shade our heads,

our daughter, strong
in heart, lovely in mind,

rise to survive us.
I who praise

strong fire, fierce fire,
wife of my youth.

Even in darkness.
Survivors. Fellow travelers.

From Twenty-Five

Squall

For twenty miles we drove along
    the edge of a storm, blue sky above
    snow slanting hard from the west.

The road itself, winding along the river valley,
    swirls in white, a tornado of flurries,
    snow pounding on the windshield;

yellow lines and black surface
    now dim, now dissolved.

How we managed to stay just on the edge,
    never quite emerging from the squalls,
    always in sight of clearing—

How we slipped past ghost cars, pick-ups plying
    the same wintery fog, keeping their channels,
is beyond all chance and consolation.

As I drive, what lies ahead
    seems, somehow, necessary;
    and the blue sky, the blue sky—

a constant, like hope itself.

From Twenty-Five

Valentine's Day Poem
(with moon)

I adore you as men through the ages
    have adored the moon:

        because she is there,

        because she is beautiful,

        because inexplicably she tugs on the heart,
           makes me at once happy
             and sorry,

        because in a life with such darkness,
    such long shadows, you shed a little light,
my companion on these dark paths.

From Twenty-Five

October 16

the late wind and night air
arrives bearing frost
shaking its white seeds

the corn in the field
is black and rustling
like pebbles in brown sacks

soon it will be winter
the voice of a woman with child
calls out in the black air

I rise in the solid predawn
make coffee and sit
in a circle of light at the kitchen table

trying again to read a future
in the mug
or the wood's holy grain

From Twenty-Five

Pilgrimage

1.   I slide my fingers along your spine
along the row of knots
counting, losing count

once a flutter
this child
now shifts like plates of the earth's crust

houses collapse
dogs cower and whine

2.   I trace ribs north & south
from the horizon of your spine

with almost no pressure, no friction
on your skin I feel the roughness of my hands

the hard bones in the palm
the wintertorn and splintered fingers

I do not tread muscle
I cannot ease fatigue within marrow

3.   you shift.
           I realize
       you are crying

       this child this hermit
       touches nerves

       & when she travels she travels hard

From Twenty-Five

Eight months

before dawn now
you find yourself awake

listening to your body
to the baby you carry

tending to the insistence
of a life apart

can she have learned already
that from your wholeness

she too must demand
a world of her own?

From Twenty-Five

Summit

At the foot of the hill
bearing Llanstephan castle,
steel posts halt cars.
A steep gravel path winds away
through trees, a field, on up.

Five months with child
my wife takes the hill slowly,
stopping each hundred yards,
holding my sleeve, catching
her wind again. Above us,

the ruins. Remains of a gate house,
corner towers, breached walls,
kitchen, chapel; old stones
beneath sun and season
like residual bitterness.

Generations change. Shouts of children
echo across lichen-mapped stones,
cries of blood. The English, the Welsh—
a rifted family. Towers still
overlook the sea:

All ships
entering the Towy
can be spotted, markings read,
landings forestalled, invasions
repulsed. Before the English.

At the castle she sits
to rest her legs, to stop
the throbbing, to fill her
lungs with Welsh air, imagining
what freedom must have meant, and means.

From Twenty-Five

Spark

Even wooden matches
must be gripped
near their volatile heads,

and struck nearly flat
across the rough strip
like a small plane touching down.

The trick is to bring it in low,
evenly, to prevent break up—

yet aggressively, the sharp gritty touch
blooming, a small sun.

The trick is to risk being burned
in that sudden explosion—
so lovely, so necessary—to risk

friction, sudden heat, life itself,
love. To risk hastening
one's own bright ruin.

From Twenty-Five

After the Quarrel

From a great distance the flames rising over the city
appear in the night sky
like the continual setting of the sun.

You stand by the window so that the ruddy heat of the sky
outlines your head and shoulders
as if the glow rose from your skin.

The thought that you are being consumed
snaps at my heart. Forgive me.
I love you

from a heart so dark
it may survive anything
but these fires.

From Twenty-Five

Pencil Sketch

my love
we know the imperceptible pulse
the faint blood
the understatement of black
and white

lips lovely only
as they part to smile
or whisper

desire burdens each stroke
the brow heavy with thought
eyes ponderous

what can there be
between us?
so much
depends on nuance

the pencil traces countless
concentric circles
whose interpretation appears to be
incurable happiness

From Twenty-Five

? ? ?

She lies where I left her
curled around my warm spot in the bed
soon to move closer
like a hand closing
as the bed, slowly, cools.

She wakes, later, cold
to find me sitting beside the radiator
fingers warmed by a coffee mug
in layers of sweaters,
preparing for day.

Why is she so cold
without me?

or I
in the days
following the winter births of our sons,
unable to heat the blankets alone
through those infirm nights?

Some design, no doubt,
that once paired
in youth
we grow steadily incapable
of holding heat alone

and in the effort
slowly curl
into the form
of a question.

From Twenty-five

The Way of Love

While in my heart I wish it were not so,
The infant given life will grow and leave.
Love is only love that lets love go.

If fate controls tomorrow, what can I know?
Flight prefigures in madness to conceive—
Still, my heart regrets that it be so.

What I believe is not enough, I know.
I tender love. Soon, in time, I shall grieve.
Love is only love that lets love go.

We reach for life above the fray, but live below.
Shall flesh remain as mind has taken leave?
How often I have wished it were not so.

Our love exceeds what comfort words bestow.
One clings to what one can though life deceive.
Love is only love that lets love go.

Though good intentions only bring me low
The infant given life must stand and leave.
Still, while my heart insists it be not so:
Love is only love that love lets go.

from The Gifts of Formal Verse

A Note for your Bathroom Mirror

lay your head down
my friend
and let the day tumble
off in the dark
let those wrinkled worries
ease

I have gone again
while you sleep as
you must
be still my heart

there is nothing I miss
so much
as lying beside you in your stillness
there is nothing made
that reins my anger
as your human
calm

a time will come again
not tonight
when I shall lay myself down beside
you my soul
in my pain and your rest
and I will touch you
as with sores
to be healed

for that night
and the others
I thank God

From Twenty-Five

What Comes to Mind

the young cat prowling for mice
in the tall weeds
the grey rain at dawn
the new babe whose leaping makes you moan
as you sleep
o dark river
o mystery woman
o keeper of my heart

I wake to this:
rain
words
the black cat who has gone on
your song
so ancient
so inspired
so far beyond reach.

From Twenty-five

What God Shall Join

As sun in splendor rises,
so sun in flames shall set.

While West is west
and never East,
yet sun is never most
nor moon least.

Where "I" and "I" be joined,
the journey is not two, but one.

from The Wedding Poems & The Gifts of Formal Verse

Old Lovers

After fifty years
old lovers
is neither kind
nor apt
true as it
may be
in our
take-him-in
turn-him-out
world.

Sap still rises
in trees.
Water
rushes to the sea.
We build fires
for heat and light.
A nod
to all
the old meta-
phors, true as
they are.

From Twenty-five

A Tree of Living

1.

A tree grows in the field,
Bare of leaves, awaiting spring.

The first sun, rising from easterly hills,
Sets it aglow as if from within.

Each branch, curve and angle
Bears fire. This is marriage,

A single thing with infinite facets.
It is promise, an unfolding,

A life-surging within time,
The future beginning in this moment.

Better this handful of quietness
Than two of chaos and storm.

2.

Better too this pairing
Two become one
Than one who has no other

Here the satisfactions of one
And one are blossom, flower
And blessing, hope, new life

They are treasure and riches
Investment, God's economy
Compounded and paid out

As a sun both warms and illuminates
Two, twin, mistress and master
Two chambered heart

To constrain when constraint is needed
To bear and be born
To be courage and encouragement

To encourage, to be-friend, to companion
To know and be known, to lie down
In peace and rise together in joy

3.

Even so,
one is how you
came to the world,
one is how you shall leave.
Yet between joy
and sorrowing,
there shall be
bold companionship,
a tree that stands
in this field, lit by first light,
a burning bush,
God's promise made
visible, a beacon
this marriage of true souls,
radiant in every limb,
every feature filled
by heavenly power
come now to earth.

From The Wedding Poems

In Medias Res

The poet regards the mirror formed by words
of his own making, and what he sees is fracture, reflections
that appear variously as trees and water;
as topography lined and chaotic with isobars;

as moments that vanish when they appear;
as the faces of his children or of others
who become his children; as the angelic
face of his beloved, honored in medias res;

as—in its own obsessive gravity—the face
behind the face he shows the world; as
—in flashes—as if he had somehow caught the sun—
burning glimpses of God that blind him

that bring him fumbling back to study its
depths. And to sing. Again. And again.

From Ash & Embers

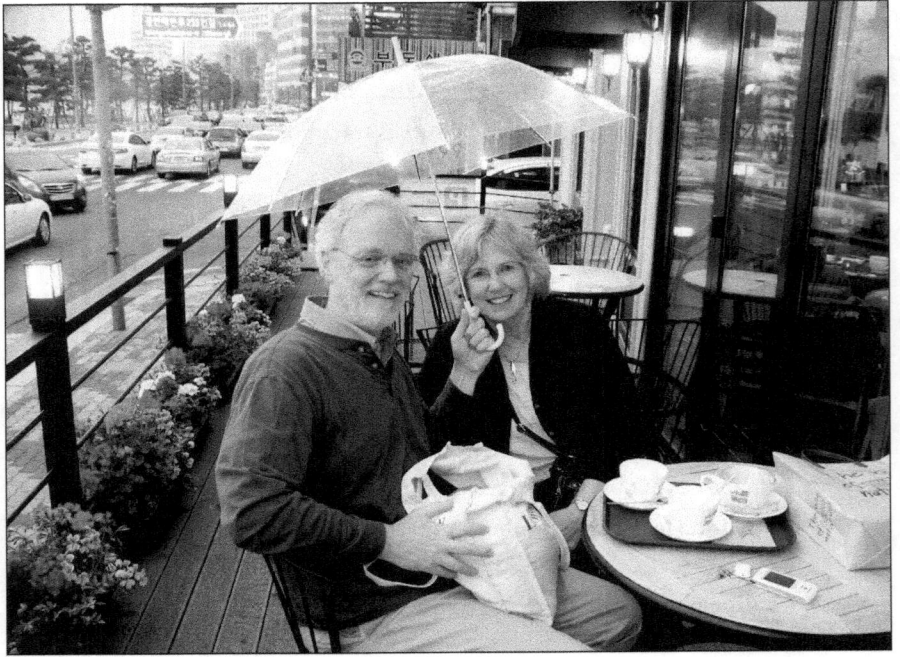

Valentine's Day (2018)

Although no one asks
to see our side-by-side
spin move
and though we have
the energy of chia pets
these days
you are still my
gold medal!

from Cards Made to Reference Life

An Early October Occasion

I have brought you this leaf
because I thought it was beautiful
and I wanted you to share that beauty.

It is a small gesture to convey, I hope,
love. In itself the leaf tells us
that God is sovereign—even as life brings its changes.

It is a unique message in a world, a natural world,
teaming with unique messages.
Its colors—green center shifting to yellow
and tinged with red—are a reminder of its life,

its life rhythms, its seasonal changes.
And like all these natural gifts, we must enjoy it
in the moment we are given.

from The Boy's Pile of Ordinary Wonders

The Idiom[3] of Marriage

I. Heritage

A late spring morning, I imagine,
resembles the garden at Creation,
sky washed the blue of robin's egg
by rains before dawn.

I imagine Father, God, at leisure,
early sunlight slanting among trees,
water on each leaf blasting light—
light lining each limb and trunk,

light demanding shadow—like day,
night—light itself visibly sifting
among leaves, cast chaotically
among its million shades, brilliant on the path.

I imagine God breathing deeply
the air of damp grass and cedar bark,
the heaviness of rain dampened soil,
the promising odor of leaf rot and punk wood.

Affirmation and Response

Marriage, my daughter and my son, is the soil you thrive in:
    A poor city dweller must live by his wits.
    Those who live on the soil have no want of plenty.

---

3. An expression having a meaning that cannot be understood from the literal meanings of its elements.

Those with food enough don't imagine they are poor.

[Response] *As it has been, so it is. So it shall be.*

Marriage, bridegroom and bride, is the soil you tend and pass along:
    Marriage is your hope, your future, your
    inheritance, your real place. As soil must be tended,
    worked and rested, prepared and weeded, used and
    enriched, so marriage. It is your vocation.

    It will sustain you. Flourish. It is your heritage
    to your children and to theirs.

[Response]*Let His people say, Amen. Praise God.*

II. Mystery

All metaphors accrue:[4]

    oneness as well as otherness
    left hand and right hand, one body
    great ring with neither beginning nor end
    what will be and what was—
        dawn and dusk and what lies between
        high noon and midnight, darkness and light
        May and October, the seasons of man

All metaphors build and give shape:

    marriage is brilliant sun crowning the eastern hills
        the promise in the rainbow
    farmer and field, the fertile fields of life
        care of soil and mule
        both plow and furrow

4. to increase or accumulate over time; a gain thereby

vine and branch, graft and rootstock

All metaphors form of what we know:

confined by what we know
collide and reconfigure what we know—
marriage is theme and variation, overture and movement

marriage is the house set on high ground
a refuge and a beacon
built today and tomorrow and all tomorrows

you, young man and woman, are its timbers and shingles
God is its architect and the great stone foundation
we who love you are its builders with you
are its carpenters and masons

marriage is a clearing in the forest
a bridge across the flood
a lamp for the dark paths of today and tomorrow
a measure by which we plumb yesterday
marriage is the stone that sharpens steel
the steel that sharpens steel

All metaphors accrue:

the One and the Other
the one: Christ as head of His body

the other: Christ as bridegroom—
believers, together, as bride, as mystery
marriage is compost for soil, salt for meat
this and that, once and always

all things but never nothing

in a world full of shadow and night

marriage is a house built on high ground
light on a hill

III. Litany[5] and Blessing

Marriage, my children, is the soil you were sown in:
    In love were you conceived and love is your example.
    Not the wild thing that grows along the roadside
    nor the pest that overruns fields, that squanders harvest,
    marriage is your example—parents who loved each other
    and God and you, your grandparents, uncles and aunts,
    the family of God in its varieties

[Response] *So it has been. Amen.*

Marriage, young brother and young sister, is the soil you grow in:
    Rain and sunlight, manure and cultivation.
    Man and woman toil. Let God bring the increase.

[Response] *As it has been, so it is.*

Marriage, young man and young woman, is the soil you delight in:
    As all good things come from God, know
    that marriage and its benefits are of God's making.

[Response] *It is just so. God is good.*

*

God, perhaps, closing His eyes
the better to see His universe in details,
to hear macaw and cricket and elephant,

5. A prayer consisting of petitions recited by a leader alternating with responses from the assembled witnesses; a repetitive recital.

to better know His creation born of chaos

and wisdom, an order of infinite possibility,
of inevitable paradox, fragile and tough
by turns, at once tough and fragile, God's
marriage for His man and His woman—

tendril and taproot, both, created especially,
created paradoxically one and one,
brought together to form one of two.
In the beginning God imagined a future.

I imagine God in His large humor
raising us all from soil to farm soil,
to wear flannel and denim and boots,
to be tillers and herders, to tend,

to prune, to plant, to harvest,
to husband this good creation,
to nurture its life and be nurtured,
paired partnered parenting forever unparted.

In the beginning God imagines a future.
Thus, begins the long labor.

from The Wedding Poems

What Was True Is True

what is true now
was true then

the carpet bears
the marks of passage

at every door
entrance and egress

the marks of living
at every couch and chair

each replaced and
repositioned for the

weight of resting feet
seldom at rest

at every budding season
or turning of leaves

the carpet is shifted
an accommodation

to revitalize
to redistribute wear

*

so we know that
fifty is just an obvious detail

for observers
for us it is this

life lived
fabric and color

emerging patterns
that carry their own

rich awareness
their own sensitivities

*

thus one might regard
the girl in the photograph

with new vividness
and her boy with

eagerness that has
not diminished

what was true then
is true still

from notebook entries On the Prospects of Aging with You

On Marriage

You will look up one morning
from grey dishwater
to that sodden field, half-turned,

half winter-dead,
mud-furrowed and corn-stumped,
tractor mired to its hubs

beneath a sodden sky—
and you will say
"that's enough."

You will think
there is no end to the waters
wearying your hands

you who came from
higher ground from
drier ground.

What will you do then,
you who have chosen—
will you choose again?

Here is my advice, I
who have seen such fields
as mud, as dust, as winter-rock:

We are made from such things.

The land will be here tomorrow
and tomorrow—as will the dying,
the being born, the in-between.

The land demands
a long commitment.
And you who have words,

you with this small window
this sodden view
this field metaphor—

when you take your hands
from the grey water
you will dry them.

And that will feel right.
Remember how already
frost has left the ground.

Imagine the shape of summer.
Call it forth, you
who know the truth of sunlight.

Call into being dazzling greens
and here, where you can see them
tulips, blood red.

From the Vault of Misfiled Poems, under "Remedies for Discouragement"

Winter Apples

We have known the seasonal joys:
how the sun lingers with us and promises
ease of limb, and greening to every horizon—

and plans laid out like gardens—how hope
itself is a reasonable contingency. And, yes,
the work has been hard, but it is gainful work.

And then without notice the days begin
to measure themselves, the boundless sunlight
growing cautious of late sunrise and early light-fall.

Boundaries and measures make sense to the sensible.
Without our knowing, we learn cause and constraint.
Now, always, there is more to do. But we don't mind

because the toddling ones learn to walk steady;
they learn to weigh and grow strong against the day
when nights advance and cold-tempered winds hammer in.

Now that, too, is our weather. What we once loved
for its wild over-bearing has been pared to essentials
by practice and by some larger need. Thus, we

are sustained by memory
and by hopes we have laid away,
by love that owns its own goodness.

From the Vault of Misfiled Poems

A Valentine's Poem

Valentine's Day
comes once a year

You come along
once in forever

Be mine

from Red Construction Paper Taped to our Bedroom Wall

A Few After-Words

What constitutes a love poem? What makes a good marriage? How can one explain fifty years of amiable, loving, committed companionship that carries no caveats and no regrets? How can one enumerate, let alone explain, the legion shapes and shades and manifestations by which love reveals itself?

There are many partial answers to these questions, but no simple, comprehensive, or fool-proof straight-on answers. Words make for rude and fragmented efforts. I cannot relate answers that will suggest how a marriage might work *unless* those answers include commitment, effort, humor, regularly renewed motivation, a considerable measure of selflessness, flexibility (especially to engage in give-and-take), openness to the need to adapt and to change, constancy, forgiveness, a desire to see with and through the other's *eyes*, daily renewal, prayer, and God's Grace. In short, what I have to offer through these poems, though sincere and deeply felt, is inevitably partial, insufficient.

We did not speculate and could not have imagined what life would look like for us fifty years down the road when we decided to take each other on and journey together. Today was light years into the future. But we knew what commitment might mean. Fifty years later we have been fortunate enough to see it enacted, embodied, bearing fruit.

The years along the way have brought a multitude of revelations, affirmations, and blessings. Our marriage has been a work of love that God has enacted *in, for, with,* and *through* us.

One result of our journey is family—four children, four spouses, and ten grandchildren.

Another result of this journey involves the poems in this book, *An Angel of the First Degree.* The poems concerned with the larger family are collected elsewhere, in *Simple Clutter*, in *Living on the Flood Plain*, in *Ash & Embers*—as well as, one hopes, in books still being made.

These *Angel* poems are all, significantly, love poems.

Many of the poems are incidental in that they just appeared in the busyness of life, *the way many things appear in the busyness of life.* Some began as a way to describe the joys of everydayness. Some have been a means, necessary for me, of directing and expressing emotion that, as we say, must "find an outlet." In this category, I suppose, are the Valentine's Day poems, which are, or can be, both earnest *and* light-hearted. Culturally, Valentine's Day poems as found in greeting cards and "love poem anthologies" tend toward the formulaic and superficial. Not so here. However much I may have made use of the traditional Valentine's Day formulae, these small poems are intended to *use* the formula rather than to repeat them, to push beyond the superficial, to create and express meaningful significance with the form.

Twenty-five of these poems incorporated here were collected and printed for our twenty-fifth anniversary (1995). It was called, simply, *Twenty-five: Love Poems.*

Some of those twenty-fifth anniversary poems and some of the remaining poems have appeared in my three published books, *Simple Clutter*, *Living on the Flood Plain*, and *Ash & Embers*. Other poems have been performed at weddings, and a few have remained uncollected until now in folders and boxes of manuscripts. Others, indeed, are still warm from composition.

The wedding poems form a category by themselves. Some have been performed, as noted above, at one or another wedding ceremony, for which printed copies were distributed to those gathered to witness the ceremony in hopes that seeing the poem being performed would contribute to greater insight and engagement. Others were not performed but were written in celebration and commemoration. All were written for specific people and with greater purpose in mind.

The wedding poems are included here because it is my profound belief and contention that they arise from my own experience with marriage. They could not have been written and they would not comprise honest aspirations for marriage had they not been grounded in my own experience, in my own marriage to the woman who is the subject, object, and primary reader of these poems.

Thus, all these marriage poems must be read as love poems for my lifelong friend and intimate companion, the mother of my children, my guardian angel, the love of my life. In a very real sense, one can't know me without also knowing her. We two have become one.

God has been good.

—*JAZ, 2020*

Notes on the Poems and Photographs

Cover Photo: "The Angel," public art in Islington, North London, UK.

Photo: Jim and Donna, Teenagers, Dover, NH

Photo: Busan, Moon, Dawn

Poem: "Marriage: Prelude, Mystery, & Riddles" was written for friends JooYeup and KoEun. The images and references arise from Busan, Republic of Korea.

Poem: The epigraph to "The Evil Rose" is from a version of "Jim's All Night Diner," James Tate.

Photo: Falling Water, Earthen Jar, Brick Wall at Splendid China, Shengzhen

Poem: "Let the Earth Be Silent No More" was written for son Ian and Kristen.

Poem: "The Classroom" was written for Donna to acknowledge the profound selflessness of her teaching.

Photo: Stone Wall, Busan

Poem: "On the Occasion of Marriage" was written for son Stefan and Rachael.

Photo: Sunset Triptik, Nantucket

Poem: "On Your Marriage" was written for son Dylan and Julie.

Photo: Sitting Angel

Poem: "Summit" was written during a summer trip to Wales many years ago while Donna was carrying our youngest.

Photo: Thistle, Islington, North London

Photo: 98 Aberdeen, our home in Islington, North London

Photo: Lilies, Umbiquan Graduate Student Dorm, our home in Busan

Poem: "A Note for Your Bathroom Mirror" was written during my grad school years when I had to rise at 2:30 a.m. several times a week to drive to my 8 a.m. class four hours from home.

Poem: "What God Shall Join" was written for friends JooYoung and JaeHo. The poem was intended to approximate the traditional Korean form *Sijo*. For this book I have broken the traditional form and syllable count to make the poem more accessible.

Photo: Gyeongbokgung Palace, Seoul

Poem: "A Tree of Living" was written for a former student's wedding.

Photo: Lunching outdoors in the rain with friends JooYeop and Koeun, Busan

Poem: "In Medias Res" is Latin for "in the middle of things."

Poem: "Valentine's Day (2018)" coincided more or less with the end of the 2018 Winter Olympics.

Photo: Leaves, Henrietta, New York

Poem: "The Idiom of Marriage" was written for daughter Kaitlin and Jeffrey.

Photo: Camellia, Busan

Poem: "On Marriage" was written for a former student who expressed concern that she would grow bored with farm life long term.

Photo: YuYin Hill House, Nancun Town, Guangzhou